Islamophobia and racism in America

Oscar McDougal

Contents

Introduction

Two interconnected and extremely distressing occurrences have persisted in the variegated fabric of American history, casting a long and gloomy shadow on the principles of equality and justice. Islamophobia and racism, in many forms, have afflicted American culture, affecting individuals' lives and moulding the nation's collective conscience. This book tries to untangle the tangled web of Islamophobia and racism in America, tracing their historical roots, assessing modern forms, and shedding light on the devastating consequences they have on people and communities.

Islamophobia, defined as an unreasonable fear, prejudice, or discrimination towards Islam and its followers, has a long history in the United States. From the antebellum interactions with Muslim slave populations to the present-day ramifications of geopolitical events, the view of Muslims and Islam has been damaged by misunderstandings, prejudices, and a misleading depiction in media narratives. The goal of this book is to examine the origins and history of Islamophobia in America, as well as the sociopolitical reasons that have contributed to its persistence and the effect it has on the lives of Muslim Americans.

Along with Islamophobia, racism has been a problem in America since its foundation. Racism has a long history in American culture, defined by institutional discrimination, racial violence, and persistent inequality. Slavery and segregation, as well as modern-day expressions of structural racism, have had a profound influence on minority communities, sustaining inequities in education, employment, housing, and access to justice. This book tries to give a full knowledge of the varied nature of racism and its entanglement with religion, especially Islam, by exploring the historical backdrop of racism in America.

This book serves two functions. To begin, it seeks to draw awareness on the experiences and hardships of Muslim Americans who endure both Islamophobia and racism while negotiating the complicated nexus of religious and racial prejudice. This book tries to highlight the negative impact of Islamophobia and racism on individual lives and communal cohesiveness by investigating the repercussions of these phenomena on Muslim Americans in areas such as education, employment, and physical and psychological well-being.

Second, this book tries to critically examine the role of many players in countering Islamophobia and racism, including the government, law enforcement agencies, and civil society. The book attempts to provide insights and recommendations for developing a more inclusive and equitable society by examining the success of current policies, initiatives, and grassroots movements. Education, awareness campaigns, interfaith conversation, advocacy, and action will be investigated as possible means of combatting Islamophobia and racism and establishing a culture that values diversity, justice, and equality.

As we travel through the complex landscape of Islamophobia and racism in America, let us strive to challenge dominant narratives, confront biases, and work toward a society in which all individuals, regardless of race or religion, can thrive and contribute fully to the collective American experience. We might expect to build a more inclusive and peaceful future for future generations by understanding the historical foundations and present expressions of these difficulties.

Chapter 1

The Historical Roots of Islamophobia and Racism in America

The origins of Islamophobia and racism in America may be traced back to the country's founding. Slavery, colonization, and empire left a significant impression on American culture, influencing views about race and religion that continue to this day.

Muslim slaves were transported to America from West Africa during the antebellum period, when they were typically forcefully converted to Christianity and robbed of their cultural and religious identities. This erasure of Muslim identity has persisted over the ages, with preconceptions and misunderstandings about Islam and Muslims perpetuated by the media and popular culture.

The 1979 Iranian Revolution was a watershed moment in American perceptions of Muslims, with the media presenting the event as a confrontation between Islam and the West. The 1993 World Trade Center bombing and the 9/11 attacks solidified America's poor depiction of Muslims, resulting in an increase in Islamophobic attitudes and policy.

Racism in America has a similarly lengthy and complicated history, with slavery of African people playing a significant role in the formation of racial stereotypes and discrimination. The Jim Crow period, which imposed segregation and discrimination against African Americans, lasted until the 1960s Civil Rights Movement.

Despite legal advances toward racial equality, structural racism endures in America, with minority groups still suffering from inequities in education, employment, housing, and access to justice. The Black Lives Matter movement has refocused attention on police violence and racial profiling, emphasizing America's continuous battle for racial justice.

The confluence of Islamophobia and racism is most visible in the experiences of Muslim Americans, who confront discrimination on the basis of both their faith and their race. The tactics of the "War on Terror" have targeted Muslim Americans, resulting in heightened monitoring, incarceration, and deportation. Furthermore, Muslim Americans of color experience much more prejudice and marginalization as a result of their race.

Finally, the historical origins of Islamophobia and racism in the United States are complicated and multidimensional, with centuries of institutional oppression and prejudice affecting views toward race and religion. Understanding this history is critical for addressing these concerns and creating a more equal and inclusive society.

Chapter 2

Islamophobia and Racism's Impact on Muslim Americans

Islamophobia and racism have a major and far-reaching influence on Muslim Americans' life, impacting everything from job and education to social relationships and personal safety.

Muslim Americans endure job discrimination, with research indicating that they are less likely to be employed or promoted than their non-Muslim colleagues. They also have greater rates of unemployment and underemployment, and many are compelled to work in positions that do not match their credentials owing to prejudice.

Due to their faith and ethnicity, Muslim American adolescents experience bullying, harassment, and exclusion from extracurricular activities at school. They also report feeling alone and unsupported by school personnel, which results in poorer academic progress and increased dropout rates.

Islamophobia and racism have a profound influence on the mental health of Muslim Americans. Muslim Americans had greater rates of anxiety, sadness, and post-traumatic stress disorder (PTSD) than the overall population, according to research. They also report feeling continually watched, which leads to paranoia and distrust.

Muslim Americans' physical safety is likewise jeopardized as a result of Islamophobic and racist beliefs. In recent years, there has been a rise in hate crimes against Muslims, with many occurrences targeting Muslim women who wear hijabs or other religious garb. Muslims in the United States are also subjected to heightened surveillance and harassment in airports and other public places, contributing to sentiments of dread and insecurity.

Islamophobia and racism have a huge effect on Muslim American families. Many Muslim American families describe feeling separated from their communities and culturally dislocated. They are also subjected to heightened monitoring from law enforcement and government entities, leading to distrust and terror.

To summarize, Islamophobia and racism have a tremendous and far-reaching influence on Muslim Americans, impacting every area of their life. Recognizing and addressing these concerns is critical for society to develop a more equal and inclusive society for everyone.

Chapter 3

Combating Islamophobia and Racism in America

While Islamophobia and racism have a huge effect on Muslim Americans, there are efforts that may be done to counteract these concerns and build a more inclusive community.

Combating Islamophobia and racism requires education and awareness. Individuals may be educated about the rich history and variety of Muslim Americans, which can assist to break down prejudices and foster understanding. Schools and institutions may also create anti-bullying initiatives and provide assistance to Muslim American students.

The role of the media in combating Islamophobia and racism is equally critical. The media has the ability to alter popular opinion and sentiments regarding Muslims in the United States. We can counter negative perceptions and promote inclusion by supporting varied and truthful depictions of Muslim Americans in the media.

It is the role of political leaders and politicians to combat Islamophobia and racism via legislation and policy reforms. This involves enacting hate crime legislation to protect Muslim Americans, as well as encouraging diversity and inclusion in government institutions and departments.

Combating Islamophobia and racism also requires community outreach and involvement. Building links between Muslim American and other groups may help to improve understanding and lessen prejudice. Interfaith talks, community gatherings, and cultural exchanges may all help to make society more inclusive.

Finally, people must take action against Islamophobia and racism in their everyday lives. Speaking up against discriminatory behavior, supporting Muslim American-owned companies, and actively seeking out varied ideas and experiences are all examples of this.

To summarize, combating Islamophobia and racism in the United States requires a multifaceted strategy that includes education, media representation, governmental reforms, community engagement, and individual action. We can build a more equal and inclusive society for everybody if we work together.

Chapter 4

Supporting Muslim American Communities

In the United States, Muslim American communities have encountered several problems, including discrimination, marginalization, and exclusion. Several initiatives may be done to fight these concerns and help Muslim American communities.

One critical option is to give resources and assistance to Muslim American companies and entrepreneurs. Access to finance, mentoring programs, and networking possibilities are all part of this. We can stimulate economic development and generate additional employment possibilities in these neighborhoods by assisting Muslim American companies.

Another critical tactic is to give Muslim Americans with access to healthcare and social services. This involves ensuring that healthcare staff are culturally competent and attentive to Muslim patients' requirements, as well as offering language interpretation and mental health assistance.

Education is also an important part in assisting Muslim American communities. This involves fostering diversity and inclusion in schools and institutions, as well as giving access to educational materials and events that highlight Muslim Americans' rich history and culture.

Community organizations and advocacy groups are critical in assisting Muslim American communities. Individuals suffering discrimination or harassment may turn to these groups for legal aid, advocacy, and support. They may also assist to bridge the gap between Muslim American and other groups, encouraging understanding and inclusiveness.

Finally, people must demonstrate their support for Muslim American communities via their actions and words. Speaking up against discriminatory conduct, attending community activities, and actively seeking out other ideas and experiences are all examples of this.

Finally, assisting Muslim American communities necessitates a multifaceted approach that includes providing resources and support to businesses and entrepreneurs, ensuring access to healthcare and social services, promoting education and inclusivity, establishing community organizations and advocacy groups, and demonstrating support through individual actions. We can build a more equal and inclusive society for everybody if we work together.

Chapter 5

Addressing Islamophobia in America

Islamophobia is a sort of prejudice and discrimination towards Muslims and Islam. It has become a widespread problem in the United States, with detrimental consequences for Muslim American groups. There are numerous ways that may be used to combat Islamophobia.

One significant tactic is to raise awareness and education about Islam and Muslim American groups. This involves giving factual information about Islam and its teachings, as well as honoring Muslim Americans' contributions and successes throughout history. We can challenge prejudices and misunderstandings about Islam and Muslim Americans by fostering knowledge and awareness.

Another key method is to make people and organizations responsible for their Islamophobic actions. This includes condemning hate speech, discriminatory policies, and violent attacks against Muslim Americans. It also entails collaborating with law enforcement to investigate and prosecute hate crimes.

Media portrayal is also critical in combating Islamophobia. This involves encouraging varied depiction of Muslim Americans in media venues such as news publications, television programs, and movies. It also entails holding media sources responsible for propagating Islamophobia and contesting bad images of Muslims and Islam in the media.

Another essential technique for combating Islamophobia is community participation. Building connections between Muslim American groups and other communities, encouraging communication and understanding, and generating possibilities for collaboration and cooperation are all part of this effort. It also entails encouraging Muslim communities in the United States to advocate for their rights and actively engage in civic life.

Finally, structural concerns that lead to Islamophobia, such as racism, xenophobia, and discrimination, must be addressed. Advocating for policies that promote equality and justice for everyone, as well as opposing policies that perpetuate inequality and injustice, is part of this.

To summarize, addressing Islamophobia necessitates a multifaceted approach that includes promoting education and awareness, holding individuals and organizations accountable who engage in Islamophobic behavior, promoting diverse representation in media, engaging in community outreach, and addressing systemic issues. We can build a more equitable and inclusive society for everybody if we work together.

Chapter 6

Supporting Muslim American Communities

Discrimination, harassment, and hate crimes have all been experienced by Muslim American populations. There are numerous techniques that may be done to help these communities.

One critical tactic is to give services and assistance to Muslim Americans and their families who have faced prejudice or harassment. This includes legal assistance, therapy, and community engagement activities. It also entails supporting Muslim Americans' access to healthcare, education, and career opportunities.

Another critical tactic is to establish safe havens for Muslim American groups. This involves making physical locations available for religious services, community gatherings, and cultural activities. It also entails pushing policies and practices that safeguard Muslim Americans' rights and dignity in public areas.

Community involvement is also essential in assisting Muslim American communities. Building links between Muslim American groups and other communities, encouraging conversation and understanding, and generating possibilities for collaboration and cooperation are all part of this effort. It also entails encouraging Muslim communities in the United States to advocate for their rights and actively engage in civic life.

Another essential technique for assisting Muslim American communities is media coverage. This involves encouraging varied depiction of Muslim Americans in media venues such as news publications, television programs, and movies. It also entails holding media sources responsible for propagating Islamophobia and contesting bad images of Muslims and Islam in the media.

Finally, it is critical to address structural concerns that lead to Muslim American prejudice. Advocating for policies that promote equality and justice for everyone, as well as opposing policies that perpetuate inequality and injustice, is part of this.

Finally, assisting Muslim American communities requires a multifaceted strategy that includes giving resources and assistance, establishing safe places, doing community outreach, encouraging media representation, and tackling structural challenges. We can build a more equitable and inclusive society for everybody if we work together.

Chapter 7

Building Understanding Bridges

As attempts to assist Muslim American communities continue, it is becoming more vital to concentrate on developing understanding bridges across diverse populations. Chapter 7 delves into the need of encouraging discourse, empathy, and collaboration in order to create a more inclusive society.

Interfaith discussions are critical in mending the divide between Muslim Americans and individuals of other religions. Individuals may use these discussions to share their views, traditions, and experiences, promoting mutual respect and understanding. Communities may break down prejudices and build empathy among various religious groups by sponsoring interfaith activities, seminars, and debates.

Education is critical in overcoming ignorance and encouraging inclusion. Schools and educational institutions may help Muslim American communities by establishing multicultural curriculum that appropriately depict Muslim Americans' achievements throughout history. It is also critical to give teachers and staff with cultural sensitivity training so that they may establish inclusive settings and address any prejudices or misunderstandings.

Empowering young people is critical for creating a peaceful community. Establishing youth activities that promote conversation, cultural exchange, and leadership development may allow Muslim American adolescents to interact with peers from other backgrounds. These programs may help break down barriers and increase understanding among future generations by developing multicultural connections and encouraging open-mindedness.

Chapter 8

Advocacy and Political Participation

We now dig into the importance of activism and political participation in furthering the rights and well-being of Muslim American communities, building on the foundations of support and understanding.

Individuals are empowered to take action and push for change in their communities via grassroots activism. Muslim American groups may mobilize grassroots efforts to raise awareness about community concerns, organize demonstrations, and participate in community-based projects. Grassroots activists can make a concrete difference in the lives of Muslim Americans by amplifying their voices and campaigning for policies that promote equality and justice.

Political representation is critical for ensuring that Muslim American communities' opinions and concerns are addressed at all levels of government. Encouragement of Muslim Americans to run for political office, campaign funding, and the development of political networks may lead to greater representation in decision-making bodies. Having elected Muslim Americans may assist design policies that meet community concerns and contribute to a more inclusive political scene.

Chapter 9

Celebrating Diversity and Cultural Exchange

Let us now emphasize the necessity of honoring Muslim American communities' vast variety and encouraging cultural interaction as a method of fostering understanding and respect.

Organizing cultural festivals and events that highlight Muslim Americans' customs, arts, and cuisines may create opportunity for individuals of all backgrounds to learn, enjoy, and interact with the community. To promote cultural variety and develop meaningful relationships, these activities may be hosted in partnership with local groups, schools, and community centers.

Creating venues for cultural exchange and cooperation may be accomplished through forming alliances with other community groups, corporations, and institutions. Muslim American groups may help to create educational programs, exhibits, and seminars that foster intercultural understanding and appreciation by developing links with museums, libraries, colleges, and other local bodies.

Chapter 10

Maintaining Progress and Building a Better Future

We are now concentrating on maintaining the gains gained in assisting Muslim American communities and envisioning a better future for everybody.

It is critical to focus ongoing education and awareness in order to maintain development. This entails giving workshops, seminars, and trainings on a regular basis to community members, educators, and law enforcement officials in order to improve their awareness of Islam and Muslim American experiences. Misconceptions and prejudices may be addressed and demolished by keeping the debate open and ensuring correct information is communicated.

To maintain progress, coalitions and alliances with other underprivileged groups and social justice organizations must be formed. Recognizing the interdependence of diverse conflicts, Muslim American groups may band together with partners to campaign for greater social change. These alliances can elevate their combined voices and build a stronger, more inclusive movement by working together.

Investing in mentoring and leadership development programs within Muslim American communities may assure the development of future leaders who will carry on the support and advocacy work. Offering mentoring, scholarships, and professional development programs may help people become change agents in their communities and beyond.

Maintaining progress requires continued interaction with policy and law. Muslim American communities may actively engage in the political process by being educated about pertinent issues, lobbying for their interests, and collaborating with legislators to effect good change. Muslim Americans may help to create a more equal and inclusive society by influencing legislators and changing legislation.

It is critical to emphasize resilience and self-care in the face of continued action to help Muslim American communities. Individuals and communities must prioritize their well-being since advocacy and activity may be emotionally and physically draining. Promoting mental health resources, encouraging self-care habits, and developing support networks may help people maintain their energy and dedication to the cause.

Conclusion: A Joint Journey

Supporting Muslim American communities is an ongoing, collaborative endeavor that involves commitment, teamwork, and consistent effort. We may establish a society that cherishes and promotes the rights and well-being of all its members by following the ideas outlined in this book and adjusting to the changing demands of the community. We can develop empathy bridges and create a better, more inclusive future for Muslim Americans and society as a whole through discourse, understanding, and collective action.